twenty-one

Anna Haas

BookLeaf Publishing

Presentation by *BookLeaf Publishing*

Web: www.bookleafpub.com

E-mail: info@bookleafpub.com

ISBN: 9789357211567

First edition 2023

DEDICATION

thank you

mum

dad

Olivia

Sam

people without whom a layer of life would undoubtedly be missing

PREFACE

this book is for myself
and for all those who must close their eyes tight
until
they can see colour

the distance between two daffodils

the distance between two daffodils
is not rare or uncomplicated
roots may cross but their petals will never touch

as a child, i chased grasshoppers
and hand-picked fragile flowers of bare beauty
that i crushed to make perfume

gifted to family and friends
the essence of spring would go musty
in recycled spray bottles around home

a decade on
at the back of the garden
on my knees
planting peas
i dug up a goldfish coffin
once laced with a girl's tears
then forgotten and left to rot

a murder from ten years ago
by juvenile lack of care for trying

mosaic of a mother

some nights
your eyes were like two disco balls
mosaic of triangular mirrors
reflect your hidden thoughts onto the walls

then all we needed to do to understand you
was dance to the rhythm of your mind music
under your strobe lights of things hidden

little mosaic triangles of morning light
burnt onto eyelids
imprinted on the irises
of two young girls
taught to be happy with half

little mosaic triangles of tired morning
conversations
or family love
or sometimes
sadness

little mosaic triangles of butter

jam
marmite imported over
or
nutella

little mosaic triangles of time
before
we leave each other for school
for what feels like a lifetime
we are older when we get back home
and hear you ask ‘teatime?’

rainbow-sky

when i am fifteen years old
i stop
out of breath
and look up at the sky

at first i think it is blue
as you do
but look again
and i see it's made up of
millions of little rainbows
all holding hands

throwing thoughts into the river
whirlpools of my brain
swirling eddies of the week's excess
drowning in warm air

sitting on a bridge
i am talking with the birds
they ask me to sing
i am too shy

and then, it feels so completely impossible
to bother with anything other than this
when this is the most worthwhile i think i know

talking with trees
whilst sitting on a rock's knee
and feeling so completely family

and then, rain
like an army
deadening yelling
that seems to have no end or beginning

extremities not being of any importance here
the raindrop soldiers march through streets of
lined trees
of a hometown-forest

but i, apart, occupied with the birds,
watch raindrop soldiers riding tree-top leaves
rushing towards you hidden in overflowing
streams

but you and i apart
too far apart i cannot keep you dry
waiting for the storm to surrender
clouds to shrink, riverbeds to empty,
for friends to reunite
under the rainbow-sky splendour

sand and infidelity

the salt stings my face
like the aftertaste of your prickly kisses
the taste of sand and infidelity

swimming with fish
the bottom of the sea is gold with kids

sitting on a rock
water wanting to make friends
and
our hearts broken

thoughts of love
and
our heads still young

summer heat
summer haze
summer love
some are lost
and
some are found

(but that isn't important right now)

i watch an old man
must be around 80
hobble up the street with two big bags in both hands
scraping along the floor
pulling his arms way down to his knees,
stretched out, tired, and visibly shaking

i try and guess his name: i'm certain he is an Andrew
but then again, he could be more of a Martin

when all of a sudden
there is no time for it to be a question
because Andrew or Martin stops
bags dropped down onto the floor
back against the wall just before a shop

like a secret agent flat and still
with both hands stuck together in front of his chest
finger and thumb
pretend gun

i am involved now in this secret scheme

next, Andrew or Martin, peeks over into the shop-window
where an old lady, Liz or Judy, is hidden behind a mannequin
fresh white new plastic body covering old wrinkled skin
price gun behind her bum

three
two
one
and bang
the first shot
from Andrew or Martin who stepped out of cover
from outside straight to the heart
knees bent falling to the ground
she is down
but no!
Liz or Judy shoots back
and now Andrew or Martin is the victim
not bleeding blood but laughs and smiles
with angled or sometimes missing teeth

and
then they take it in turns
middle of the street

middle of the day
excellent display of not giving a crap
playing this game they play only for the other's
cheers
daylight robbery of age
stealing back years

a warm laugh i can hear echo through the
decades
the beauty coming back in flashes of reddish
cheeks
they are young now
and i can see it in their smile

two people
fresh love
who can't see the years disappearing
who never ever ever wanted to be old from the
beginning

two people who would always make fun of each
other
because back then, nothing ever would really
matter

two people who always kept the other alive
when one would have rather been dead
the other unable to create life

two people who found life easier together
just the two of them
just two people

it only lasts a few seconds
after all, they are old
they get tired
the man waves his small white handkerchief
over his head
or rather by his ear
old again

she too accepts defeat by blowing a small kiss
through the windowpane
they try and touch hands against the glass
hobble and crouch uncomfortably to get closer
but, once touching, no pain

they take their hands back leaving only two
handprints behind

i watch as Andrew or Martin
or probably neither
(but that isn't important right now)
picks up his bags and carries on up the street
before life overtakes him again
so that he can meet up with Liz or Judy's own
little life later tonight

i don’t know Andrew and Judy or maybe Martin
and Liz
yet
i felt their battle
against age
for the sake of youth and love that maybe
doesn’t have to go away

i felt their pain and years of complex life
stories and memories align to make fun where
fun can be made
by two people who are maybe just afraid

yes i am young
and, yes, i haven't played their games
and yes i don't know their names
but i know they were happy
that he didn’t kill himself
and she kept going without her baby
and i know that then, they were happy
shop window war, what for?
caught at the right time
hope
as i window-shop for something sublime

little honest hands

the little girl left
only a fairy
on the table,
made out of
bits and bobs

twigs as arms and legs,
spread out wide;
a shiny magenta coloured sweet wrapper
topped off by three delicate pink petals as a
dress;
two white ones for her shoes;
a yellow bow made out of forgotten trash
balanced on a green unripe plum head;

all laid out on the wooden table
all she left behind
her little honest hands made
the sweetest artwork

the next day, a gust of wind
blew the fairy
away, back to the land

ode to what he was

what he was?

flowers and bees
and summer
breathing secrets into each other's mouth

curves that make lines
sometimes lines that make curves

a mix of moon and sunlight
music and sugar
the sweetness of time
the fulfilment of emptiness
or is it the sweetness of emptiness
and the fulfilment of time
(uncertainty is a big part of him)

a friend
a familiar face
under multicoloured fairy-lights
and behind the softness of bedtime

rare comfort
worth the challenge

i don't know what he is really
but i know being with him
it all made sense, made music
it's a mix of courage, laughter, love and spice
magic electricity

when we fell asleep next to each other
his breath on my face
a lullaby

his presence
a good night's kiss

his closeness
the only eyewitness

he was and will stay that night

that night we danced together
our bodies collide and explode, reform and
collide
again, and again to the rhythm of the music
the colourful lights reflect from his eyes into
mine
hand touches skin, even through t-shirt
his hand is on my arm

his breath on my face - icing sugar - he laughs, i laugh
seeing each other laugh, we laugh more
it is more than laughter; it is fire coming from burning bellies
we are dragons, flying over slayers and mountains
dopamine, adrenaline and alcohol mix to make a dangerous cocktail
we rush for air outside when our hearts are on fire
when the music gets too loud, the only music we want to hear is each other's
we sit, me next to him, him next to me, just the two of us, a three-euro beer to share
i see the moon in his hair
i hear she and he slowly become them
you and me became us
you were my plain white t-shirt

in short, if i had to draw him, he would be smiling

invisible currency

calendar still on the 11th of November
a man late to being somebody
or some body late to being a man

scribbles on a note that once was played in a
game of roulette
fatigued figures on pennies, fortune rolling out
of filled pockets
in this world where accounts count, the wind
blows angry at the peculiar power of at times
invisible currency
controlling what we can or cannot see, can or
cannot be

i have a friend who is rich and a friend who is
poor they do not get along anymore

MY LAPTOP IS NOISY

MY LAPTOP IS NOISY
and it hurts my head

it's incessant thrumming bores into my brain
like a tractor on my lap
lap-top-tractor

i hate it when it stops me from sleeping
i hear it buzzing in my dreams
now
i don't speak anymore, i hum electronically

and i know that soon we will all be vibrating and
whirring too
but
some days
i miss
how beautiful
our voices
were
when
we
spoke
together
just us
in whisper

the story of you and me in raindrops

drought, drought, drought
and then thunderstorms

nothing, nothing, nothing
and then everything at once

again and always
suddenly,
vibrantly, rain
always as unexpected

suddenly,
vibrantly, life
of foolish beauty
too much for only me
or only you
or only us

eyes cutting through eyes
murderous rain determined to wet almost
everything
devastating silence in the open mouths
of two young lovers who do not know how to
love

odd fingers on paired odd bodies
the grey clouds move quickly through the sky

ears ringing with the sound of your thunder
for weeks after you've gone

walking under the rain
but it's only when i'm touching you
that i am wet, otherwise indifferent
hurricanes or drizzles
both are equally as vital and rare

the story of you and me is raindrops
scattered through the years

the story of you and me
raindrops and the permanence of instability
never knowing when i will see you again
but always knowing we are never over
a part of my breath always trapped in your lungs
a part of you always locked in my head

us, both equally see it
we know that no one compares, no one will
replace
no one will come close to who we are when we
are together

for we both keep the best versions of ourselves
for one another

but it's killing me --- it must be killing you too
and killing, yes, is the right word because i live a
little less brightly when i'm not with you

but because you are everything, you must take
everything,
and the more complete the love, the more
complete the suffering

and so even though i beg for more
even if i'm dying of thirst
i cannot take you, you cannot take me
because there would be no me and you anymore
we would be incapable of being distinct people
we would just be us, lost inside the other

the story of you and me can only ever be
in raindrops

full english in the rain

i am eating a full english in the rain
on a bench, full english in the rain
feeling fully english

i am eating a full english in the rain
is that strange?

it feels nice, different,
stumbling on something misplaced
happening upon something partially wrong

i wonder how many people have eaten a full
English in the rain?
the sausage was nice although more soggy than
you'd want it
no crisp in the rain

the beans got too wet,
drops sitting between bean and sauce
i did not finish them

how oddly satisfying to know what this
unusuality feels like
to know something that by pure coincidence was
a secret to the rest of the world until now

i think i'll do it again soon

when you take up the whole sky

i can't find moon tonight
i ask around
no one can tell me where
she's gone
again

so i shout out
useless words into the sky
like every time moon disappears

moon, help, i can't see you
moon, help, are you okay?
moon, sun will be here soon
moon, tell me if you're still my friend
cause you've been gone for days and I've been worried

she shows herself
slips out from behind a grey night cloud
wearing nothing
looking thin

moon, not again, you can't
moon, you've gone all small
moon, have you been eating at all?

sure enough
moon had not
starving herself so that she looks like a curved
needle
shining white bone pulling from beneath her
damaged skin

moon, we've talked about this
moon, why do you hurt yourself?
moon, you're beautiful when your full
moon, why do you hurt yourself?
moon, everybody admires you when you take up
the whole sky

moon was beautiful
but moon just couldn't see it
moon hated her body
constantly changing from full to empty
impossible of being happy with any one look
permanence was the issue here

no cloud dress or star jewelry could help
she was alone with herself
alone with her hate for herself
alone to think she wasn't beautiful
alone to think she wasn't beautiful

so i say goodbye with the usual sentence

moon, please, eat something tonight

the storm

memories
as sharp as
the edges
of your face

memories of you,
the storm

you, the storm

the storm that made every wave
beg to be broken by you

the storm that demanded more raindrops
from the eyes of frightened girls flooding empty
streets

the storm that needs
to be watched in the darkness

with no mercy
you whisper to the sky

"you'll never wear your blue dress again"

and there, and then - and now, here

and there
no
was
no
where
to
be
found

and then,
she knows
his rude ways
will outstay their
welcome

and now, here,
the only thing she feels that
she has in common with
who she was that night
is the little voice
inside of her

begging

please stop

help us up next time

it happened
because a messy group of boys would throw
pennies at my 15-year-old sister's ass on her
way home

it happened
because an adolescent's dirty hand stained my
16-year-old thigh under the desk at school

it happened
because his ignorant friends watched at 17 when
i was too drunk to stop him myself

it happened
because strangers felt they were entitled to touch
my mother on a train when she was 18 and
asleep

it happens and has happened to every woman in
my family
because a man believes he can because others
are

it happens

because when i fell
i wanted someone to pick
me up
not force their warm dick
into my mouth

made to feel like that was unreasonable of me - I
was drunk on confidence after all

it is happening

and it will keep happening
until there is understanding of how they leave us
hollowed out

help us up next time

platform conversations

just a look, and a look back, eye contact of 0.7
seconds,
scared but she doesn't show it

she walks out to the very end of the concrete
island that separates the two train tracks
to get away from him

but that means she is alone now, and he sees it
and he follows her or follows it, maybe that's
how he sees her

without looking she can feel him too close
'hiya' he says, not to her face
but to her body,
to her curves
her newly washed hair
her legs that look thin
in her new pair of jeans
her boobs
her bum
her memories
her fears
her twin screaming on the inside 'get away from
me'

but not to her face

‘hello’ she says back through closed lips (to his
face)
recognising the drunk saggy red-black eyes but
still not showing the fear

he sits down on the bench next to her but it feels
like he is
in her
already
after all, she knows what it's like, she knows
what's coming

alarm bells are ringing
all the sirens are going off
all is shouting and screaming and yelling and
crying and
it's so noisy she can't hear herself breath
(and i can tell you, even you’d be able to hear
her breath, at night, when she’s alone)
but no one can hear her all they hear is silence

he pushes his hands down on his thighs, stands
up slowly bending himself straight
and starts moving closer towards her, if that’s
even possible
bends down in front of her, closer again, if that’s
even possible

his breath on her face

and she does show it now
she can't help it
she wants to jump in front of the oncoming train
to escape
him (him from the memories)
and this
  man   ?

his heavy 'have a good evening' blown in her
face smells like vodka
she knows the feeling, she sees his eyes
she smells his indifference towards her face but
not towards her body
his breath was the same as last time
the one that stained the carpet of her childhood
like sweet wine, like blood
the one that also smelled like vodka
and lingered in the room after he'd gone
leaving her lying alone in her own small pool of
blood, in a bed with no sheets

bending himself straight again, he walks straight
past her,
not straight sorry, definitely not straight,
he walks swaying past her, back towards the
station
and the relief, oh the relief

as he (it) walks away
back up the stairs and, back out the station
oh the relief

and when everything is finally done and gone
and has finished shouting and screaming and
yelling and crying and
the silence comes creeping back onto the
platform
like rabbits after a fox
she feels safe
again

for now

i didn't expect it to sting

i didn’t expect it to sting

when i scrapped at my skin with nail scissors
until it fell away like curly wood shavings
until blood came
shocking reminder of my body as living

i didn’t expect it to sting

when pain had become permanent
and rare, if not absent, the feeling of something
so strikingly different
until blood came
until the places their hands had touched
were swollen and agape

i didn’t expect it to sting
or for it to hurt when i walk
or for it to hurt in my sleep
or for the paranoid pin and needle pain to be
palpable

a moment where i was so far away
so far removed from my own body
that control was only possible through attack

vivid attack
violent attack
visible attack

i had to see what my mind
had been doing to my girlhood for years
cutting it open
with nail scissors
until blood came

but, you see, i didn’t expect it to sting
for i did not expect to feel anything
faith found in blood came
with nail scissors
faith swollen and agape

perhaps foolish
perhaps shocking
certainly faith
for i felt it sting

a poet unmuted

your ability to be indifferent when you see me
cry
is harsh
but my inability to write about you
is worse

a poet silenced by the distress of two
people who don't add up
panic is discovering we may not share
enough of one another for me to find any poetry
in us

your ability to be indifferent when you see me
cry
is harsh
but my inability to write about you
is worse

a poet silenced by the distress of two
people who don't add up
betrayal is knowing that one look and i
could write a whole book about someone else

your ability to be indifferent when you see me
cry
is harsh
but my inability to write about you
is worse

a poet silenced by the distress of two
people who don't add up
rebirth is unmuting a broken voice
censored so as to please you, for too long

your ability to be indifferent when you see me
cry
is harsh
but my inability to write about you
is worse

a woman silenced by the oppression of a man
who's always on top

freedom was understanding you'd never believe
in what i stand up for

your ability to be indifferent when you see me
cry
is harsh

but my inability to write about you
is worse

a girl, she was just a girl

my ability to be indifferent when i see myself
cry
is harsh
but my inability to love
is worse

my ability to be indifferent when I see myself
cry
is harsh
but my inability to cut you out of the poem is
worse

my ability to write
my inability to think

my ability to write
our inability to love

your ability to be indifferent when you see me
cry
is harsh
but my inability to write about you

is worse

a poet silenced by the distress of two people who don't add up
what do you do when there is no beauty left?
what do you do when there are no rhymes?
what do you do when you two have no rhythm left?
what do you do when you can't erase the words?

your ability to be indifferent when you see me cry
is harsh
but my inability to write about you
is worse

a poet unmuted by the distress of two people who don't add up

we are not repeating this again
you are not repeating this again
i am not repeating this again
i am women
i am author
i am poem
i am what comes after the next full stop.

my ability to be beautiful is astonishing

my ability to be beautiful is astonishing
you should not be threatened
by the ease with which i am

pretty women are
pretty male gaze ruin
your life is of sexier safety

this morning,
singing in the shower
dancing under the water
making esteam i'm so on fire!

passion fruits of particular passion
i look damn good
but i smell even better
my mind and all it's complications slipping
around the wet tiles of the bathroom floor
bubbles under armpits

i'm not running after it
not now (i'm busy dancing remember)
kick it around from time to time
i'll catch it later

hips swaying
shoulders popping
womanhood glowing with a smile
bouncing up and down
feeling both
lost
and
found

powerful
proud

busy being my own best friend
busy being my own lover
busy owning my own company
busy being whatever the fuck i wanna be
in my own fucking shower

thank you

the day after i fell in love with you
i am the girl sat on the beach listening
to the noise of bees at work
birdshine and sunsongs
(everything about you becoming a mix and a
muddle)
trying to make sense of you
trying to make sense of us
thinking of you so much
that to lose you would be to lose my mind

all i am sure of
is that your skin was soft

poetry on palms
letters scribbled on cheeks by fingertips
trying to say "i love you"

since then
i am the girl who found home
in the pockets of your jacket,
in the grace of your blue eyes,
and the lyrics of our bodies
sung to the playlists you create for each month

i am the girl who tries to explain how love is not
enough
i love flowers
i love the stars
i love sleep and chocolate
i love the white dog
under a tree
that always was and always will be bigger than
me
but you are more than love
you are years of pain condensed into a tear
allowed to roll free down a cheek
you are the beauty of kindness encapsulated in
one man
you give my world a new layer of meaning

i am the girl whose name you say
like it's the amen of the religious people

i am the girl whose body you paint
drawn with your fingers, eyes closed
like you're rubbing out where i go wrong and
sketching me right

i am the girl in who you plant flowers
gardener devoted to his earth
by my side as they grow from seeds to trees

we are lips
pressure
on wounds

we are eyes
placing laughter
into the other's heart

we are games
puzzles and competition
and playing until you let me win

we are hands
on the horizon
of our bodies
and our minds

i am the girl, turned women, who can only say
thank you
to the boy, turned man, that you are

how to give a loved one back to the earth

how to give a loved one back to the earth
was the question on everyone's mind

the seagulls flying low
the rushed river seemed less rushed today

yellow screwdriver unscrewing screws on the
wooden box
holding life, bones, wrists, a wedding ring, and a
handbag

each person taking a handful of mum
or a handful of grandma
or a handful of woman admired and loved
taking the piece of her they knew
the tune of "Salley Gardens" in heads
each spreading out in their own direction
corners of garden and edges of river
scattering handfuls of her
across the wall, down the steps
her slipping through tightly clasped fingers

into every crevasse, onto every stone, onto every leaf

the sun was warm on our backs
our palms white from powdered ash

down by the river, she glistened
as the water took her from our cupped hands

the lighter parts of her washed away
the heavier parts sank to rest among the stones

part of her in the air
part of her laying on the riverbed

soon little black fish appeared
and she was already part of something bigger

a blending of happy and sad
a blending of life and death
seeing others cry and crying together

flowers float down the river in procession
a white butterfly, a bumble bee

freesias once in a wedding bouquet

now in a pile on green grass

we discuss the water cycle
and that a part of her will undoubtedly end up
back in Kashmir

we joke that there is still a lot of her left
and there is
for everyone, everywhere, every day

we think about what she would say
we laugh

we walk along waterloo street
carrying some of her in hand, all of her in heart

memories of her dropping from hands to cobbles
she knew well
steps she had walked a thousand times

from the bridge, we let go of the petals of her
life
and on my leaning shoulder, she laid her caring
hand
tears heavy for generations of childhoods made
joyful

as one last gift
he came to meet her, after all this time
a vision of a kingfisher they knew was real
a dad, a grandad, once was a man
a flash of blue, then brown copper, then gone
a part of him in another form
him and her, molecules always and still attracted
both now onto the next part of their journey
death reincarnated into forever

we think to ourselves
ashes to ashes
dust to dust
here to gone
treasured as ours
now back to the earth

www.ingramcontent.com/pod-product-compliance
Lightning Source LLC
Chambersburg PA
CBHW051738130826
49812CB00033B/913
9789357211567